Spanning two millennia of thought, quotes from various religions, cultures, ideals, and understandings are presented. These quotes are not endorsed as being either correct or incorrect, but rather, are meant to make the reader stop and ponder. Hopefully, after experiencing this small collection, the reader will also have re-evaluated some of his or her own thought patterns and belief structures.

The goal of this project is to point out that neither time nor space creates any true, lasting divisions or barriers – only the human mind can choose to hold on to separation or limits, as opposed to the concept of unity.

If you, dear reader, come across a statement that initially seems to go against your current worldview, ask yourself, "Why? What is it about this particular statement that is triggering me?" If you feel defensive about a particular idea, try to understand the underlying reason(s) for it. Likewise, if you embrace a particular view, inquire as to why this thought resonates.

If read in such a manner, I believe readers will gain a greater understanding of their own inner workings and those of their fellow beings, creating greater empathy and an increase in (their level of) compassion.

Compassion, being of a very high vibration, holds tremendous potential for the manifestation of anything the soul desires. Within these pages are glimpses and tools others have found helpful on their own path.

I wish you well on your journey.
Yvette Farkas
Toronto, Canada, 1998

Table of contents:

CHARACTER OBSERVATIONS & EGO 1

THOUGHTS & OBSERVATIONS 15

CONSCIOUSNESS, ENERGY & ALTERED STATES 39

DEATH, DYING, & LIVING 51

SUGGESTED LITERATURE: 60

SUGGESTED AUTHORS: 63

"Our deepest fear is not that we are inadequate. Our deepest fear is that we are powerful beyond measure. It is our light, not our darkness that most frightens us. We ask ourselves, Who am I to be brilliant, gorgeous, talented, fabulous? Actually, who are you not to be? You are a child of God. Your playing small does not serve the world.

There is nothing enlightened about shrinking so that other people won't feel insecure around you. We are all meant to shine, as children do. We were born to make manifest the glory of God that is within us. It's not just in some of us; it's in everyone.

And as we let our own light shine, we unconsciously give other people permission to do the same. As we are liberated from our own fear, our presence automatically liberates others."

-Marianne Williamson-

CHARACTER OBSERVATIONS & EGO

We must be the change, We wish to see in the world.
-Mahatma Gandhi-

As long as the intellect has not accepted or decided a thing completely, it often becomes impossible to speak or act.
-Swami Vyas Dev Ji- "First Steps to Higher Yoga"

To conceal truth (knowledge) Is mental theft.
-Swami Vyas Dev Ji- "First Steps to Higher Yoga"

When lecturing, if one deliberately does not properly explain a point and evades giving full answers or steals the thoughts of others, or expresses contrary to what he has seen or heard; It is theft.
-Swami Vyas Dev Ji- "First Steps to Higher Yoga"

Nobody steals what belongs to him.
-Swami Vyas Dev Ji- "First Steps to Higher Yoga"
Do nothing – but intelligently.
-Ayurveda class of 96-

You will become your environment – control it, or you will manifest it
-Ayurveda class of 96-

Wisdom is simply allowing
-Maya Tiwari- "Secrets of Healing"

Neither promise yourself things nor do things if you see that when deprived of them, they will cause you material suffering.
-Leonardo Da Vinci-

One who, being freed from externalities, Is master of himself.
-Eido Tai Shimano & Kogetsu Tani-
"Zen Word/Zen Calligraphy"

We try to control, to change things to how we want them. This can be done to a certain degree but cannot be done completely and eternally. If, on the other hand, we accept things as they are and see things as clearly revealed as they are, that acceptance is the first step toward unbreakable peacefulness.
-Eido Tai Shimano & Kogetsu Tani- "Zen Word/Zen Calligraphy"

We have a tendency to do something with the expectation that we will be compensated. There is a doer and a receiver, and in between, there is compensation. But in the world of oneness, there is no giver, receiver, no donation. There is just pure doing and, therefore, no expectation and no disappointment.
-Eido Tai Shimano & Kogetsu Tani- "Zen Word/Zen Calligraphy"

Oh, what a tangled web we weave, when first we practice to deceive.
-Sir Walter Scott-

Are you up to your own destiny?
-Hamlet- " William Shakespeare"

The external life of an individual could appear highly ascetic and austere to others, but all the while, it would be profoundly happy. The fact is th at the real sage is anything but ascetic; however, he may appear to be so to the sensual man.
-Franklin Merrel-Wolff- "Pathway Through to Space"

Remove the cause or deal with the issue.
-Ayurveda class of 1998-

As soon as you accept the designations of race, gender, name, or fellowship, you define yourself in contrast to the Tao.
-Deng Ming-Dao- "365 Tao"

Egotism does not manifest solely in the form of conceit. It can also be traced in most humility, for the inferiority complex is as much a phase of egotism as is the superiority complex.
-Franklin Merrel-Wolff- "Pathways Through to Space"

In Buddhism, this return to nirvana is connected with a complete extinction of the ego, which, like the world, is only an illusion. If nirvana may not be explained as death cessation, still, it is strictly transcendent. In Taoism, on the other hand, the goal is to preserve in a transfigured form the idea of the person, the "traces" left by experience.

-Translation by Richard Wilhelm- "The Secret of the Golden Flower: A Chinese Book Of Life."

Now I'll be quiet and let silence separate what is true from what are lies, as threshing does.
-Rumi- "These Branching Moments"

"Could I whisper in your ear a dream I've had? You're the only one I 've told this to." He tilts his head, laughing, as if, "I know the trick you're hatching, but go ahead."
-Rumi- "These Branching Moments"

Man reflects just what he seeks.
-Franklin Merrel-Wolff- "Pathways Through to Space"

Thus, unfinished "good" karma is as truly a source of bondage as unfinished "bad" karma. The really vital point to note is that it is not action, whether "good or bad," that frees, but an attitude of detachment with respect to all action.
-Franklin Merrel-Wolff- "Pathways Through to Space"

The joy that invariably accompanies mystic experience (or any other kind of ego loss) is simply the natural emotion that wells up when this sense of fearful isolation ends.
-Andrew Weil- "The Natural Mind"

There is an important idea in Nietzsche of "amor fati," the "love of your fate," which is, in fact, your life. As he says, if

you say no to a single factor in your life, you have unravelled the whole thing.
-Joseph Campbell- "The Power of Myth"

How can you fool him? The melodrama of the ego is not going to fool the divine beloved. You can fool human beloveds with the melodrama of the ego because it is largely what they want. They want this massive soap opera to go on and on. But the divine beloved is doing nothing except burning in total love waiting for you to become total love.
-Andrew Harvey- (on Rumi) "The Way of Passion"

To find and be the rose, you have to give up trying to understand. You have to give up trying to know anything. You have to give up all the ego's desires to control the experience.
-Andrew Harvey- (on Rumi) "The Way of Passion"

The fire has to enter the log, but the log is damp and covered with grimy, old, dank moss – I am so depressed, my mother abused me, I lost my job, I lost 17 girlfriends in a row, I want to kill myself, the world is ending, I am just sick of the whole experience, I want to die – that is the damp, dank log that we all identify with, that is the ego, the endless whining, self-piteous, dreary voice that goes on and on. What happens first is purification, to get back to the Sufi theme. Purification is frightening because in the fire there is a lot of black smoke, a lot of difficulty happens. Then expansion, the fire enters the log and the light enters. You burn in the fire, and the blaze is without interference

Shh – no more words... Hear only the voice within.
-Andrew Harvey- (on Rumi) "The Way of Passion"

Nothing breeds appropriate behavior faster than exposure to the light of public scrutiny.
-Neale Donald Walsh- "Conversations with God"

Deny nothing, simply observe what is so, and what works.
-Neale Donald Walsh- "Conversations with God"

The way to control your thoughts is to change your perspective.
-Neale Donald Walsh- "Conversations with God"

I cannot give you what you do not believe you may have, no matter how much you desire it.
-Neale Donald Walsh- "Conversations with God"

As long as I am seeking something, I cannot have it, because my very seeking is a statement that I do not have it.
-Neale Donald Walsh- "Conversations with God"

Life begins at the end of your comfort zone. Nothing is painful, which is understood and is not real.
-Neale Donald Walsh- "Conversations with God"

The biological imperative is not to create more life, but to exchange that life as it really is: A manifestation of I-ness.
-Neale Donald Walsh- "Conversations with God"

now because the impurities have been burnt away. The blaze is there, this great sunburst of the illumination of bliss, which is the second stage. But this is not the final stage. The final stage can never be talked about, and no one, not even Rumi, has ever described it. The divine mystery is ringed about with silence at the end, and only the lover can go into the bedroom of silence. It is the last moment when the fire is dying, and the love is ash, an amazing soft, deeply tender, deeply radiant glow emanating from the log. This is union, this is oneness, because this is a love so empty and so tender that the entire universe is always dancing in it; Nirvana, Moksha, Baqa, Liberation, Now.

-Andrew Harvey- (on Rumi) "The Way of Passion"

The mystery of union begins when longing has softened you up enough to receive the tenderness of the beloved. The mystery of union begins when you have been destroyed enough to be grateful for a blade of grass. For the wind, and the freshness of the morning, for a beautiful face on the bus. Because at that moment, you're beginning to see that you are in a divine world, surrounded by mercy. But how stripped do you have to be to receive the mercy? To arrive at that point when you suddenly begin to see the miracle of everything around you, you have to lose all the false miracles of the ego. You have to die for the life which is trembling in everything around you to appear in its full circle.

-Andrew Harvey- (on Rumi) "The Way of Passion"

You teach what you have to learn.
-Neale Donald Walsh- "Conversations with God"

Explain to me, please, why sincerity is so important in giving to another what you choose for yourself. If you give to another as a contrivance, a manipulation meant to get something to come to you, your mind knows this. You've just given it a signal that you do not now have this. And since the universe is nothing but a big copying machine, reproducing your thought in physical form, that will be your experience. That is, you will continue to experience "not having it" – no matter what you do!
-Neale Donald Walsh- "Conversations with God"

Doesn't this make fate a kind of anarchy? A continuing war among principalities? Yes, as it is in life itself. Even in our minds - when it comes to making a decision, there will be a war. Acting in relationship with other people, for example, there may be four or five possibilities. The influence of the dominant divinity in my mind will be what determines my decision. If my guiding divinity is brutal, my decision will be brutal as well.
-Joseph Campbell- "The Power of Myth"

Just as sheer life cannot be said to have a purpose, because look at all the different purposes it has all over the place, but each incarnation, you might say, has a potentiality. And the mission of life is to live that potentiality. How do you do it? My answer is, "Follow your bliss." There's something inside you that knows when you're in the center, that knows when you're on the beam or off

the beam. And if you get off the beam to earn money, you've lost your life. And if you stay in the center and don't get any money, you still have your bliss.
-Joseph Campbell- "The Power of Myth"

There is nothing wrong with having nothing to say – unless you insist on saying it!
-Unknown-

In highly evolved societies, no member of those societies is ever judged and found guilty of anything. They are simply observed to have done something, and the outcome of their actions, the impact of them, is made clear to them. Then they are allowed to decide what, if anything, they wish to do with regard to that. And others in the society are allowed to decide what, if anything, they wish to do with regard to that. They do nothing to another. The idea of punishment is simply not something that occurs to them, because the concept of punishment itself is incomprehensible to them. Why would the "one being" want to hurt itself? Even if it has done something damaging, why would it want to hurt itself again? How does hurting itself once more correct the damage of the first hurt? It's like stubbing one's toe, then kicking twice as hard to retaliate. Of course, in a society that does not see itself as one, and does not see itself as one with God, this analogy would not make sense. In such a society, judgment would make perfect sense. Judgment is not the same as observation. An observation is a simple looking, a simple seeing of what is so. Judgment, on the other hand, is a concluding that something else must be so because of what is observed. Observing is witnessing, judging is concluding.

-Neale Donald Walsh- "Conversations with God"

Forgiveness is experienced only in young, primitive cultures. Advanced cultures have no need for it, understanding that, since there can be no damage, no forgiveness is necessary.

-Neale Donald Walsh- "Conversations with God"

Think how it is to have a conversation with an embryo. You might say, "The world outside is vast and intricate. There are wheat fields and mountain passes, and orchards. At night, there are millions of galaxies, and in sunlight the beauty of friends dancing at a wedding." You ask the embryo why he, or she, stays cooped up in the dark with eyes closed. Listen to the answer. There is no "other world." I only know what I've experienced. You must be hallucinating.

-Coleman Barks- "The Essential Rumi"

Learning martial arts means self-assurance, not arrogance. Your confidence should make you the meekest, most humble person on earth. If you are secure in your techniques, nothing anyone can do has any meaning. It is impossible for them to annoy you because you know they cannot harm you. You know you can fight, but you do not exercise that ability. You remain free of violence.

-Deng Ming-Dao- "Chronicles of the Tao"

I am not advocating blind self-denial. Pure asceticism can be mentally and physically dangerous if it is unbalanced. Vegetarianism without the tonic herbs to balance is wrong. Celibacy without technique is insane. This is the test of

your mastery: How do you attain balance? You must always ask yourself this.
-Deng Ming-Dao- "Chronicles of the Tao"

The heart of the perfect man is pure. Even in a swamp he remains unsullied. Though thunderstorms destroy mountains, and winds churn the four oceans, he is unafraid. He flies through the clouds, sails above the sun and moon, and transcends the world. His heart is with all things, but he is not one of them.
-Deng Ming-Dao- "Chronicles of the Tao"

Good manners without sincerity are like a beautiful dead lady. Straightforwardness without civility is like a surgeon's knife; effective but unpleasant. Candor, with courtesy, is helpful and admirable.
-Paramahansa Yogananda- "Autobiography of a Yogi"
The iron filings of karma are attracted only where a magnet of the personal ego exists.
-Paramahansa Yogananda- "Autobiography of a Yogi"

The modesty of which he wore his scientific fame repeatedly reminded me of the trees that bend low with the burden of ripening fruits; it is the barren tree that lifts its head high in an empty boast.
-Paramahansa Yogananda- "Autobiography of a Yogi"

To see a world in a grain of sand, and a Heaven in a wild flower, hold infinity in the palm of your hand, and eternity in an hour.

-William Blake- "Auguries of Innocence"

There are only two ways to live your life. One is as if nothing is a miracle. The other as if everything is.
-Albert Einstein-

Character cannot be developed in ease and quiet. Only through experience of trial and suffering can the soul be strengthened, vision cleared, ambition inspired, and success achieved.
-Helen Keller-

Eternity is not in the hereafter. This is it. If you don't get it here, you won't get it anywhere.
-Joseph Campbell-

When you are in a state of awe, you're in a persistent state of gratitude. Perhaps the surest way to happiness and fulfillment in life is to thank and praise your source for everything that happens to you. Then, even when a calamity arises, you can be assured that you'll turn it into a blessing.
-Dr. Wayne Dyer- "The Power of Intention"

The power of intention is paradoxically experienced by what you are willing to give to others. I love Swami Sivananda's advice, and I encourage you to consider it here. Everything he suggests, you own in infinite amounts. The best thing to give your enemy is forgiveness. To an opponent, tolerance. To a friend, your heart. To your child, a good example. To your father, deference. To your

mother, conduct that will make her proud of you. To yourself, respect. To all men, charity.
-Dr. Wayne Dyer- "The Power of Intention"

Discarding doubt is a decision to reconnect to your original self. This is the mark of people who live self-actualized lives. They think in no-limit, infinite ways. One of the no-limit qualities is the ability to think and act as if what they'd like is already present.
-Dr. Wayne Dyer- "The Power of Intention"

Detach from the outcome. Don't let your authentic and peaceful attitude depend on your relative's behavior. As long as you remain connected to intention and radiate outward high energy, you've achieved your peace. It's not your place or your purpose to make everyone else in your family think, feel, and believe as you do. By letting go, you guarantee your own peace, and you dramatically increase the odds of helping others to do the same.
-Dr. Wayne Dyer- "The Power of Intention"

THOUGHTS & OBSERVATIONS

Truth is one. The sages speak of it by many names.
-Joseph Campbell- "Hero with a Thousand Faces"

The differences of sex, age, and occupation are not essential to our character, but mere costumes (masks) which we wear for a time on the stage of the world. The image of man within is not to be confounded with the garments. Such designations do not tell what it is to be a man. They denote only the (accidentals) of geography, birth, date, and income.
-Joseph Campbell- "Hero with a Thousand Faces"

Striving makes little sense when one is already united with the object of one's striving.
-Joseph Campbell- "Hero with a Thousand Faces"

The transmission of the archetype is unaffected by the symbol transmitting it.
-Joseph Campbell- "Hero with a Thousand Faces"

The individual not qualified for use of this (knowledge) is protected by a lack of interest, or a deficiency of understanding, so that such literature seems either uninteresting or meaningless to him.
-Franklin Merrel-Wolff- "Pathways Through to Space"

As we grow by interacting with our soul mates, we ascend the ladder of lifetimes. We transcend old patterns, come to fully experience love and joy, and love every vestige of anger and fear. Eventually, we come to a point where we

can voluntarily choose to be reborn to help others directly or even choose to stay in spirit form and help others from another level. Reincarnation for emotional growth is then no longer necessary.
-Brian Weiss- "Through Time into Healing"

Often the soul returns to a new lifetime with the same talents and abilities a person exhibited in a previous lifetime. Sometimes, people even access unknown talents in a current lifetime. There are so many levels of self. We are wonderful, multidimensional beings. Why must we limit ourselves mentally by restricting our definition of ourselves to the personality and body that exists in the here and now? The entire spirit is not encapsulated in the body and conscious mind. The part of the self which exists here, is in all probability, just a fragment of the entire spirit.
-Brian Weiss- "Through Time Into Healing"

There was a reason for her having chosen to experience her current lifetime. Her current troubles and obstacles were not random or accidental but had been designed to accelerate her spiritual progress.
-Brian Weiss- "Through Time into Healing"

It is true that overcoming obstacles and difficulties accelerates spiritual progress. The most serious lifetime difficulties, like severe psychiatric illness or physical disability, may be signs of life progress, not regress. In my opinion, it is often the very strongest souls who have chosen to shoulder these burdens because they provide

great opportunities for growth. This is probably why difficult lifetimes are more frequently recalled during regressions. The easier lifetimes, the "rest" periods are usually not as significant.
-Brian Weiss- "Through Time Into Healing"

I am "beauty" and make all things to become beautiful. But the real "beauty" is entirely apart from the object, however subtle.
-Franklin Merrel-Wolff- "Pathways Through to Space"

Essentially it is only the shell of man that lends itself to observation by methods adapted from the physical laboratory. Behind the shell is another organization where more primary causes operate. As a consequence, in order to trace the causes which manifest as objective effects to their root(s) sources, both subtle senses and something of metaphysical understanding are requisite.
- Franklin Merrel-Wolff- "Pathways Through to Space"

Pure light is all colors, therefore, it has no hue. Only when singleness is scattered does color appear.
-Deng Ming-Dao- "365 Tao"

If all is forgotten, then nothing is learned.
-Arthur Frank-

When nothing is (no longer) compelling, What reason is there? (To live, seek, etc.).
-Abhinavagupta- (Tenth-century philosopher)

The subject creates the object due to persistence of cognition.
-Abhinavagupta- (Tenth-century philosopher)

The silence you experience between each thought is your own fullness, the same fullness that is pure consciousness.
-Swami Dayananda Saraswati-

Regardless of the form or regardless of the spiritual, psychological, and emotional conditionings, things are perfect as they are and cannot be otherwise at this moment. This is the Zen point of view.
-Eido Tai Shimano & Kogetsu Tani- "Zen Word/Zen Calligraphy"

Confucius (551 – 479 B.C.E) said, "I have nothing to hide." To say it more clearly, there is nothing that is hidden; everything is revealed as it is.
-Eido Tai Shimano & Kogetsu Tani- "Zen Word/Zen Calligraphy"

We are deceived by many tangible "existences" and think that they exist. But, after all, there is nothing, no "thing." With this understanding, we eliminate unnecessary pain caused by delusion. Indeed, not a "thing" exists.
-Eido Tai Shimano & Kogetsu Tani- "Zen Word/Zen Calligraphy"

People may interpret selflessness as a moral and ethical term. In a way, it is a beautiful attitude to be selfless, but

Zen Buddhism is talking about realizing the fundamental reality that has no self, no entity, no element, and no particles. Rather, this endless dimensioned universe is the self itself.
-Eido Tai Shimano & Kogetsu Tani- "Zen Word/Zen Calligraphy"

Whenever we exhaust our accumulated knowledge, we speak the truth: "I know not."
-Eido Tai Shimano & Kogetsu Tani- "Zen Word/Zen Calligraphy"

Have preferences, but no needs.
-Neale Donald Walsh- "Conversations with God"

A demonstration which starts from a fount that is less than divinity, can never prove the existence of divinity.
-Franklin Merrel-Wolff- "Pathways Through to Space"

There is no such thing as true objectivity.
-Zoe Wolf-

A good master leads you to the true master within.
-Deng Ming-Dao- "365 Tao"

Peaceful calm upon the moor accepts the moonlight without care.
-Zoe Wolf-

The wild geese do not intend to cast their reflections. The water has no mind to receive their image.
-Zen Tanka-

Ah, Kankodori, deepen thou my loneliness.
-R.H Blyth- "Haiku"

(In the above haiku, "loneliness" by which is also implied "interpenetration with all things" – finds expression in a haiku about a mountain bird called the "kanko-dori" that lives far from the haunts of man and whose voice is always heard in the distance).

Scent of plum blossoms, on the misty mountain path.
-Basho-

The word "ZEN" has its roots in Yoga tradition. It evolved out of the Sanskrit word "dhyana," which means "meditation." "Dhyana" is the seventh stage of Patanjali's eight stages to enlightenment.
-J. Donald Walters- "Superconsciousness"

There is a reason for the three sounds of "OM." Each sound represents a distinct aspect of the Cosmic Vibration, out of which was produced all manifested creation. "A" is the creative vibration and is higher in pitch than the others. "U" is the vibration that maintains the universe (equilibrium). "M" dissolves creation back into spirit at the end of each cycle of cosmic manifestation, the lowest pitch. The three aspects of the Cosmic Vibration have been personified in Hindu mythology as Brahma, Vishnu, and Shiva – and woe to that rash Advaita (non- dualist) who tells the Hindu fundamentalist that these personages are only myths. In fact, so all-embracing is the beauty of the Sanatan Dharma (the Eternal Religion) that even the symbol is considered to be imbued with some of the power that it represents. A myth is real if it can bring cosmic truths to a focus.

-J. Donald Walters- "Superconsciousness"

When we humans are connected with this divinity, both here and in the afterlife, our security comes from within. When we are alienated from the divine source, we look for security outside ourselves in some form of ego gratification and energy-stealing control dramas.

-James Redfield- "The Celestine Vision"

Dreaminess is a great barrier. But most of human consciousness, even in this world, is in a sort of waking-dreaming or somnambulistic state. However, we have instruments that can shock to wakefulness. Unquestionably, pain is one of the very greatest of these instruments and thus is much less an evil than a beneficent agent. The more I have studied the problem, the more I have become convinced that it has been a great mistake to concentrate so much attention upon evil. The real difficulty is the almost universal somnambulism in which men pass most of their lives, some spending many lives without leaving this state at all. It is, in effect, a hypnotic sleep, and the real problem of religion is not the saving of human souls from evil but a dehypnotizing of the mind. So I should place somnambulism, rather than

egoism or evil, as the first among problems that must be mastered by humanity if it is to progress toward liberation.
-Franklin Merrel-Wolff- "Pathways Through to Space"

Man reflects just what he seeks.
-Franklin Merrel-Wolff- "Pathways Through to Space"

By saving yourself, you inevitably save the world.
-Joseph Campbell- "The Power of Myth"

The fisherman throws out his hook, gets the fish, and then winds it in slowly until it is exhausted. So when he actually gets the fish out of the water, as it is dancing about, in fact, it is bleeding to death. That is the joke. You think that you're evading and dancing away, that you are having a nervous breakdown, having hysterics. You are not. You are just bleeding to death. And when you get exhausted, the divine is going to reel you in . This is perfect. The hook is in your mouth. You are hooked by love and tenderness. You are hooked by divine experience. The master is just sitting there, quietly, reeling you in.
-Andrew Harvey (On Rumi) "The Way of Passion"

Shams says to Rumi, don't give me this bullshit about me being a sea of goodness or an angel. This is your game. You are being Rumi, the poet, the wordsmith, burn, and then we will talk. He says, "Silence, love is a jewel that you cannot hand over like a stone." What he means is very profound. The master is trying to give you a diamond. What you actually want is a new Chevrolet, or a new girlfriend, or boyfriend, or both, or a new figure, or a new

career. No, none of those things. None of the fake jewels. It is the diamond that the master is going to give, so everything you ask for that is not a diamond, you won't get, or you will get it only to show you that you do not want it. "Love is a jewel that cannot be handed over like a stone." Because what is being given is nothing else than divine consciousness. And what you so often want, right up into the last stage, is a trivial approximation of an approximation of divine consciousness. The master will hold out until you long enough.
-Andrew Harvey (On Rumi) "The Way of Passion"

When you long enough, the master can just breathe on your face, and you will see the divine vision. When you long enough, the divine spirit can descend in dreams and teach you directly. But until you long enough, you are still relying on your own games, fantasies and illusions, and your own very limited intelligence, and all of these have to be taken away.
-Andrew Harvey (On Rumi) "The Way of Passion"

Highly evolved beings of the universe would never "kill" another sentient being in anger. First, they would not experience anger. Second, they would not end the corporeal existence of another being without that being's permission. And third – they would never feel "attacked," even from outside their own society or species, because to feel "attacked," you have to feel that s omeone is taking something from you – your life, your loved ones, your freedom, your property, your possessions – something. And a highly evolved being would never experience that because a highly evolved being would simply give you

whatever you thought you needed so badly that you were prepared to take it by force – even if it cost the evolved being its corporeal life – because the "HEB" knows she can create everything all over again. She would quite naturally give it all away to a lesser being who did not know this. HEBS are, therefore, not martyrs, nor are they victims of anyone's "despotism." Yet, it goes beyond this. Not only is the HEB clear that he can create everything all over again, he is also clear that he doesn't have to. He is clear that he needed none of it to be happy, or to survive. He understands that he requires nothing exterior to himself and that the "himself" which he "is," has nothing to do with anything physical. Finally, the HEB understands that she and her attackers are one. She sees the attackers as a wounded part of herself. Her function in that circumstance is to heal all wounds so that the "all in one" can again know itself as it really is. Giving away all that she has would be like giving yourself an aspirin.
-Neale Donald Walsh- "Conversations with God"

The evolution of a society is measured by how well it treats the least among its members.
-Neale Donald Walsh- "Conversations with God"

Whenever there is time, there is sorrow. But this experience of sorrow moves over a sense of enduring self, which is our own true life.
-Joseph Campbell- "The Power of Myth"

No one is grown up except those free of desire.
-Coleman Barks- "The Essential Rumi"

I've said before that every craftsman searches for what's not there to practice his craft. A builder looks for a hole where the roof is caved in. A water carrier picks the empty pot, a carpenter stops at the house with no door. Workers rush toward some hint of emptiness, which they then start to fill. Their hope, though, is for emptiness, so don't think you must avoid it. It contains what you need!
-Coleman Barks- "The Essential Rumi"

Finally, I know the freedom of madness.
-Coleman Barks- "The Essential Rumi"

To a frog that's never left his pond, the ocean seems like a gamble. Look what he's given up: security, mastery of his world, and recognition! The ocean frog just shakes his head. "I can't really explain what it's like where I live, but someday, I'll take you there."
-Coleman Barks- "The Essential Rumi"

The fact is, there is no meaning to anything save the meaning you give it. Life is meaningless. That is difficult for many humans to accept, yet it is my greatest gift. By rendering life meaningless, I give you the opportunity to decide what anything and everything means. Out of your decisions, you will define yourself in relationship to anything and everything in life. 1. Nothing in my world is real. 2. The meaning of everything is the meaning I give it. 3. I am who I am, and my experience is what I say it is.
-Neale Donald Walsh- "Communion with God"

Seek not to be the recipient of anything but to be the source. That which you wish to have, cause another to have. That which you would seek to experience, cause another to experience. In so doing, you will remember that you have had these things in your possession all along. What you give, you become.
-Neale Donald Walsh- "Communion with God"

Bless your enemy, and you rob him of his ammunition.
-Florence Scovel Shinn- "The Wisdom of Florence Scovel Shinn"

One is often cured of his faults by seeing them in others
-Florence Scovel Shinn- "The Wisdom of Florence Scovel Shinn"

The simple rules are fearless faith, non-resistance, and love!
-Florence Scovel Shinn- "The Wisdom of Florence Scovel Shinn"

You attract the things that you give a great deal of thought to.
-Florence Scovel Shinn- "The Wisdom of Florence Scovel Shinn"

In every act prompted by fear lies the germ of its own defeat.
-Florence Scovel Shinn- "The Wisdom of Florence Scovel Shinn"

Every negative situation in your life is crystallized thought that has been built up out of your own vain imaginings! But these situations cannot stand the light of truth. So face the situation fearlessly.
-Florence Scovel Shinn- "The Wisdom of Florence Scovel Shinn"

People joke destructively about themselves, and the subconscious takes it seriously.
-Florence Scovel Shinn- "The Wisdom of Florence Scovel Shinn"

It goes a mighty force, but noiseless! THOUGHT, the strongest power in the universe is without a sound.
-Florence Scovel Shinn- "The Wisdom of Florence Scovel Shinn"

At the precise moment when the last "self" shall have its freedom, the creation in its totality will be reabsorbed into the primordial substance.
-Mircea Eliade- "Yoga: Immortality and Freedom"

Hope prolongs and even aggravates human misery: Only he who has lost all hope is happy, for hope is the greatest torture that exists, and despair the happiness.
-Mircea Eliade- "Yoga: Immortality and Freedom"

In sleep, you do not know if you are a man or a woman. Just as a man impersonating a woman does not become one, so the soul, impersonating both man and woman, remains

changeless. The soul is the immutable, unqualified image of God.
-Paramahansa Yogananda- "Autobiography of a Yogi"

Do not confuse understanding with a larger vocabulary. Sacred writings are beneficial in stimulating desire for inward realization if one stanza at a time is assimilated. Otherwise, continual intellectual study may result in vanity, false satisfaction, and undigested knowledge.
-Paramahansa Yogananda- "Autobiography of a Yogi"

When your conviction of a truth is not merely in your brain but in your being, you may diffidently vouch for its meaning.
-Paramahansa Yogananda- "Autobiography of a Yogi"

The mere presence of a body signifies that its existence is made possible by unfulfilled desires.
-Paramahansa Yogananda- "Autobiography of a Yogi"

Under the impact of the unfamiliar and the altogether real danger of my physical annihilation, my body had to make use of its hidden resources or die. The trick seemed to be in the truthful acceptance of the possibility that such resources exist and can be reached.
-Carlos Castenada- "The Second Ring of Power"

A warrior actually affected the outcome of events by the force of his awareness and his unbending intent.
-Carlos Castenada- "The Second Ring of Power"

Everyone's values are defined by what they will tolerate when it is done to others.
-William Greider- "One World, Ready or Not"

Each of us, as the hero of our own life, faces different earthly and spiritual challenges from which we learn lessons that allow us to evolve different, increasingly higher qualities of power. All problems, all stresses, present an opportunity for spiritual learning in which you can gain insight into the use, misuse, or misdirection of your personal power.
-Carolyn Myss- "Invisible Acts of Power"

Whatever games are played with us, we must play no games with ourselves.
-Ralph Waldo Emerson-

In the context of infinity, living any moment of your life in anything other than appreciation and love is a waste of your life energy.
-Dr. Wayne Dyer- "The Power of Intention"

It seems to me that searching for your purpose is like searching for happiness. There is no way to happiness; happiness is the way, and so it is with living your life on purpose. It's not something you find, it's how you live your life serving others, and bringing purpose to everything you do.
-Dr. Wayne Dyer- "The Power of Intention"

When you realize there is nothing lacking, The whole world belongs to you.
-Lao Tzu- "Tao Te Ching"

When I want for you, what you want for you, then I truly love you. When I want for you what I want for you, then I am loving me through you. So too, by this measure, you can determine whether others love you, and whether you love others. For love chooses naught for itself, but only seeks to make possible the choices of the beloved other.
-Neale Donald Walsh- "Conversations with God"

The more your partner loves you, the more you will feel threatened by that love, and, at the same time, afraid you will hurt your partner.
-Sondra Ray & Bob Mandel- "Birth and Relationships"

As soon as you are faced with someone who is truly your equal, and doesn't need you, but just loves you – without your having to earn that love through helping, rescuing, or protecting – then all your unresolved feelings of neediness are likely to surface.
-Sondra Ray & Bob Mandel- "Birth and Relationships"

Where there is deep love, words are virtually unnecessary. The reverse of this axiom is also true: The more words you have to use with each other, the less time you must be taking to care for each other because caring creates communication. Ultimately, all real communication is about truth. And ultimately, the only real truth is love. That is why, when love is present, so is communication. And

when communication is difficult, it is a sign that love is not fully present.
-Neale Donald Walsh- "Conversations With God"

When I feel most destroyed, I am about to grow.
-John Heider- The Tao of Leadership"

Making love is natural. Why be ashamed of it? That seems simple, but it is actually a great challenge in these complex times. Too many other layers of meaning have been imposed on sex. Religions straightjacket it, ascetics deny it, romantics glorify it, intellectuals theorize about it, and obsessives pervert it. These actions have nothing to do with lovemaking. Can we actually master the challenge of having lovemaking be open and healthy? Sex should not be used as leverage, manipulation, selfishness, or abuse. It should not be a ground for our compulsions and delusions.
-Den Ming-Dao- "365 Tao"

When you learn to give unconditionally, which is to say, love, unconditionally, then will you learn to receive unconditionally.
-Neale Donald Walsh- "Conversations with God"

Real love begins only when one person comes to know another for who they really are.
-Leonard Rebick- Article from "Eye for The Future" (Vol. 6, Nov. 3)

Unresolved issues lead us to the person who can push the buttons necessary to open up an old trauma so we can deal with it. If we are willing to examine the whys and wherefores of our attractions, they can provide great information about our issues.
-Leonard Rebick- Article from "Eye For The Future" (Vol. 6, Nov. 3)

To be enlightened is to be intimate with all things.
-Dogen-

Real happiness is virtue, and not merely an effect of virtuous living.
-Franklin Merrel-Wolff- "Pathways Through To Space"

Each friend represents a world in us, a world possibly not born until they arrive, and it is only by this meeting that a new world is born.
-Anais Nin- "Simple Abundance"

Kind words are the music of the world. They have a power which seems to be beyond natural causes.
-Anais Nin- "Simple Abundance"

No better love, than love with no object. No more satisfying work, than work with no purpose. If you could give up tricks and cleverness, That would be the cleverest trick of all.
-Rumi- "Unseen Rain: Quatrains of Rumi"

I attain more in every man's attainment. I recognize more in every man's recognition. I am delayed by every man's failure; every new facet opened by another individual man breaking through is a new facet awakened in my understanding. Thus, from this standpoint, the duality of selfishness and altruism is destroyed. In serving others, I serve myself, and in serving myself, I serve others. So I am beyond all sacrifices and choose only my greatest pleasure. Personally, I only fail in my duty when I fall short of choosing perfectly my own supreme delight. If anyone would help me, let him progress toward his own highest glory. That is the only aid from out of the world that can reach me.

-Franklin Merrel-Wolff- "Pathways Through To Space"

The abstinent run away from what they desire but carry their desires with them: When a man enters reality, he leaves his desires behind him.

-The Bhagavad Gita-

The master cannot be seduced by anything except sincerity. That is what is so terrifying about him.

-Andrew Harvey- (On Rumi) "The Way of Passion"

It is horrible to face just how little you want to live. It is horrible to face that behind all your protestations of love, there is a passion for control, that all of your ways of saying how loving you are can be ways of avoiding being destroyed to become love. You want love, but you do not want to become love. You want to be given the visions and illuminations, but you do not want to become empty

enough to receive them. You go through every conceivable game of your own darkness, of your own nature, of your own stupidity and this is "a passion so complex that all the other world passions are simple before it." In fact, you train in the other passions to be able to bear this one.
-Andrew Harvey- (On Rumi) "The Way of Passion"

Love itself is a pain, you might say – the pain of being truly alive.
-Joseph Campbell- "The Power of Myth"

If we want to see the soul in a relationship, we have to look beyond the intentions and expectations.
-Thomas Moore- "Soul Mates"

The point of a relationship is not to make us feel good, but to lead us into a profound alchemy of soul that reveals to us many of the pathways and openings that are the geography of our own destiny and potentiality.
-Thomas Moore- "Soul Mates"

It is usually the most ordinary relationships, things, items, and occurrences, which are the most treasured.
-Thomas Moore- "Soul Mates"

As with all matters of the soul, it is honoring its impulses that we find our way best into its mysteries.
-Thomas Moore- "Soul Mates"

Pain and difficulties can sometimes serve as the pathway to a new level of involvement. They do not necessarily mean that there is something inherently wrong with the relationship; on the contrary - relationship troubles may be a challenging initiation into intimacy.
-Thomas Moore- "Soul Mates"

Being stuck in a dilemma is often a sign of superficial involvement in whatever has stirred the soul. The temptation is to remain stuck, to spend hours on thought and conversation and weeks, months, and even years luxuriating in the dilemma. As long as we are thus occupied, we don't have to dare the soul's invitation to explore new territory.
-Thomas Moore- "Soul Mates"

Sexual intimacy begins with an acknowledgment of and respect for the mystery and madness of the other's sexuality, for it is only in the mystery and madness that the soul is revealed.
-Thomas Moore- "Soul Mates"

For one thing, you can't depend on what the person promises, since the soul isn't willing to be chained to intentions or even to commitments.
-Thomas Moore- "Soul Mates"

You know a person when you know the driving Spirit that shapes the person's life.
-Thomas Moore- "Soul Mates"
1. Nothing in my world is real.

2. The meaning of everything is the meaning
I give it.
3. I am who I say I am, and my experience is what I say it is.

Happiness is a decision, not an experience. Emotions are experiences that are chosen, not experiences to which you are subjected. It is fear that turns observation into judgment and judgment into anger.
-Neale Donald Walsh- "Communion with God"

Ordinary love is selfish, darkly rooted in desires and satisfactions. Divine love is without condition, without boundary, without change.
-Paramahansa Yogananda- "Autobiography of a Yogi"

Fixity of attention depends on slow breathing, quick or uneven breaths are an inevitable accompaniment of harmful emotional states: fear, lust, and anger.
-Paramahansa Yogananda- "Autobiography of a Yogi"

The karmic law requires that every wish find ultimate fulfillment. Non-spiritual desires are thus the chain that binds man to the reincarnation wheel.
-Paramahansa Yogananda- "Autobiography of a Yogi"

The power of unfulfilled desires is the root of all of man's suffering.
-Paramahansa Yogananda- "Autobiography of a Yogi"

To be unable to forgive is to live in hell, Burdened, miserable, angry. Our egos hope those at whom we are angry are living in anticipation that we will one day forgive them. But most likely, the person for whom you hold a grudge could not care less about your misery. He has moved on, and you are stuck. Forgiveness is a powerful act that is healing to you. After all, the person you resent does not have to live in your body; you do.
-Carolyn Myss- "Invisible Acts of Power"

To see what is right and not to do it Is to lack courage or principle.
-Confucius-

CONSCIOUSNESS, ENERGY & ALTERED STATES

A great Zen saying goes: "Just do it!"
-Eido Tai Shimano Kogetsu Tani- "Zen Word/Zen Calligraphy"

The realized man is freed from the karma of past actions, save the karma that has already "sprouted," and is the causal power which maintains the continuance of the current gross body.
-Franklin Merrel-Wolff- "Pathways Through To Space"

Consciousness requires a material medium, such as a brain, to bring it into material manifestation, but it requires no such medium to exist. The outward manifestation of consciousness was a potential from the beginning of creation. As the Bhagavad-Gita Gita states, "essential consciousness exists everywhere, but is forever unaffected by anything."
-J. Donald Walters- "Superconsciousness"

As consciousness moves outward from its center into material manifestation, it takes on the appearance of material limitation.
-J. Donald Walters- "Superconsciousness"

When spirit first manifested itself as cosmic creation, it projected itself outward into a state most closely resembling pure consciousness – in the form of thoughts and ideas. Vibrationless in itself, it sets part of its undifferentiated being into vibratory movement. Thus was manifested the ideational, or causal universe: Causal, because from the level of thought forms, were projected

the vibrations that made grosser levels of manifestation possible.
-J. Donald Walters- "Superconsciousness"

Differences among astral beings are understood to have nothing to do with skin color or other outward characteristics: They are entirely a matter of individual vibrations.
-J. Donald Walters- "Superconsciousness"

It is said that even Gods consider the experience of the material world a blessing, for it grounds the understanding and enables the soul thereby to evolve more quickly toward the highest wisdom. Truths often have to be brought "down to Earth" before they can be fully understood.
-J. Donald Walters- "Superconsciousness"

Everything in the universe exists in its present state or form as the result of past causes and, in its turn, is the cause of future states of the universe. Because of the interdependence of parts, it is impossible to know completely the karma of any part without knowing all that is to be known of the universe.
-Franklin Merrel-Wolff- "Pathways Through To Space"

Take "chance" as if it had been your intention. With that, you evoke the participation of your will.
-Joseph Campbell- "The Power of Myth"

It had always seemed to me possible that through hypnosis, for example, or autohypnosis, by means of systematic meditation, or by taking the appropriate drug, I might so change my ordinary mode of consciousness as to be able to know, from the inside, what the visionary, the medium, the mystic were talking about

-Aldous Huxley- "Door of Perception"

My desire to try mescaline once I had learned of its existence was as natural as my desire to whirl myself into dizziness, hallucinate while falling asleep, sniff cleaning fluid, or get drunk in high school. I did not take mescaline because I went to Harvard, met Timothy Leary, rebelled against my parents, was amotivated, or sought escape from reality. I took it because I was a normal American teenager whose curiosity had survived thirteen years of American education.

-Andrew Weil- "The Natural Mind"

Primarily, we need more information about altered states of consciousness. Altered from what? That is a good first question. The answer is: From ordinary waking consciousness, which is "normal" only in the strict sense of "statistically most frequent." There is no connotation of "good," "worthwhile," or "healthy." Sleep and daydreaming are examples of altered states of consciousness, as are trance, hypnosis, meditation, general anaesthesia, delirium, psychosis, mystic rapture, and the various chemical "highs."

-Andrew Weil- "The Natural Mind"

Trance, whether spontaneous or induced by a hypnotist, is simply an extension of the daydreaming state in which awareness is focused and, often, directed inward rather than outward.

-Andrew Weil- "The Natural Mind"

Another chief characteristic of all these states is a major change in the sense of ego, that is, in awareness of oneself as a distinct entity. Thus, when we catch ourselves daydreaming, we wonder where we were for the past few minutes. Now it is most interesting (to note) that many systems of mind development and many religions encourage their adherents to "forget" themselves in precisely this sense. For example, in Zen archery, the meditating archer obliterates the distinction between himself and the bow – hitting the bull's eye with the arrow then becomes no more difficult than reaching out and touching it, and the shot is always a bull's eye. T.D. Suzuki, who brought Zen to the attention of the West, has written of this process: "The archer ceases to be conscious of himself as one who is engaged in hitting the bull's eye which confronts him." In fact, the ability to forget oneself as the doer seems to be the essence of mastery of any skill. And since the observing ego is the center of normal waking consciousness, the essence of this kind of mastery of any skill is the ability to forsake any kind of consciousness at will.

-Andrew Weil- "The Natural Mind"

The risk of negative psychosis is something to be taken into account. But, just as in the case of the panic reaction, this risk is inherent in the individual, NOT the external trigger. Psychosis does not come packaged in joints of marihuana, tablets of LSD, or spoons of cocaine. Rather, people are variously susceptible to develop negative psychosis under stress.

-Andrew Weil- "The Natural Mind"

Careful study of Eastern literature, however, shows that yogis and Buddhists are strictly concerned with practicalities. Continued alteration of consciousness by means of drugs, they say, ultimately makes it harder for individuals to attain and maintain the most worthwhile states of altered consciousness. Their reasoning is clear: Drug experience strongly reinforces the illusion that highs come from the external material things rather than from one's own nervous system. And it is PRECISELY THIS ILLUSION that one strives to overcome by means of meditation. Long before I understood this point of view, I had made an interesting clinical observation. I noticed that all persons I met who were visibly dependent on drugs, whose lives were ruled by their habits, thought about drugs in a particular way. They were convinced that the experiences they enjoyed came in the joints of marihuana, tabs of acid, or shots of heroin, and they saw NO OTHER way of getting them. There is no doubt in my mind that drug dependence is ESSENTIALLY AN ERROR OF THINKING, NOT a pharmacological or biochemical phenomenon, even though it may be accompanied by changes in the physical body. And it makes no difference whether the drug is marihuana, heroin, or alcohol; the error in the mind is always the same.

-Andrew Weil- "The Natural Mind"

People who think that experiences come from drugs eventually find that drugs begin not to work as well for them. This subjective tolerance to experience seems clearly related to an illusory way of thinking because people who see through this illusion solve the problem of tolerance whereas people who do not are overcome by it. The person who begins to notice that acid (or aspirin) no longer puts his head in the right place as well as it used to has a choice. He can begin to look for other methods of getting to that place and may discover that meditation is such a method, or he can pursue the experience through the drug more and more desperately. In the former case, he will evolve away from drugs in his continuing explorations of altered states of consciousness. In the latter case, he will become involved with drugs in a more and more neurotic manner and eventually will become less free to use his nervous system in interesting ways. These considerations explain why the highs of meditation are universally perceived as better than drug highs. Drug experience includes many extraneous phenomena that are quite irrelevant to the (desired) state of consciousness. (E.g., Dilated eyes, cold hands...) The experience is an indirect effect coming from the mind in response to this physiological trigger. It never occurs to many drug takers that the two aspects of the drug experience are separable and that the high can be had without its physiological trappings. But the first time one achieves such separation, the superiority of pure high uncontaminated by physiological "noise" is obvious. The trouble is that drugs seem to work powerfully and immediately, whereas meditation requires persistence and effort. But the results are worth it.

-Andrew Weil- "The Natural Mind"

Various states of consciousness are extremely complex products of Prakriti.
-Mircea Eliade- "Yoga: Immortality and Freedom"

Liberation is only a "becoming conscious" of its eternal freedom.
-Mircea Eliade- "Yoga: Immortality and Freedom"

The coordination of a synchronistic event requires an enormous amount of energy. You increase the frequency of synchronistic experiences in your life if you make it a practice to live in the present time. As a medical intuitive, I have learned that people who are stuck in the past are hampered In their ability to live and make decisions. They can't retrieve their energy from their history, and their lack of energy keeps their minds, bodies, and spirits from working together; it also makes them slower to heal. To have your spirit spread out across forty years of history, still "processing" experiences that are decades old, drains your life force. I call this "psychic weight," and the more you have in your mind and heart, the longer you have to "wait" for things to happen in your life, including spontaneous forms of assistance coming to you when you need it. When your past Is more alive and real to you than the present, synchronistic events are less likely to come together if for no other reason than you lack the power to recognize them or take advantage of their appearance.
-Carolyn Myss- "Invisible Acts of Power"

Spirit works to awaken us, and it seems that If we don't pay attention to the subtle messages, the messages increase in volume and severity.
-Carolyn Myss- "Invisible Acts of Power"

The spiritual journey does not consist in arriving at a new destination where a person gains what he did not have or becomes what he is not. It consists in the dissipation of one's own ignorance concerning one's Self and life and the gradual growth of that understanding which begins the spiritual awakening. The finding of God is coming to one's Self.
-Aldous Huxley-

The way to establish a relationship with spirit and access the power of this creating principle is to continuously contemplate yourself as being surrounded by the conditions you wish to produce.
-Dr. Wayne Dyer- "The Power of Intention"

We attract to us that which we emanate.
-Dr. Wayne Dyer- "The Power of Intention"

What you are feeling is a function of what you are thinking, what you are contemplating, and how your inner speech is being formulated.
-Dr. Wayne Dyer- "The Power of Intention"

Stop being offended. The behavior of others isn't a reason to be immobilized. That which offends you only weakens

you. If you're looking for occasions to be offended, you'll find them at every turn. This is your ego at work convincing you that the world shouldn't be the way it is. But you can become an appreciator of life and match up with the universal intention of creation. You can't reach the power of intention by being offended. By all means, act to eradicate the horrors of this world, which emanate from massive ego identification, but stay in peace. Being offended creates the same destructive energy that offended you in the first place and leads to attack, counterattack, and war.
-Dr. Wayne Dyer- "The Power of Intention"

Let go of your need to be superior. True nobility isn't about being better than someone else. It's about being better than you used to be. Stay focused on your growth with a constant awareness that no one on this planet is any better than anyone else. We all have a mission to realize our intended essence; all that we need to fulfill our destiny is available to us. None of this is possible when you see yourself as superior to others. When you project feelings of superiority, that's what you get back, leading to resentments and, ultimately, hostile feelings.
-Dr. Wayne Dyer- "The Power of Intention"

Why is everyone here so happy except me? "Because they have learned to see goodness and beauty everywhere," said the master. Why don't I see goodness and beauty everywhere? "Because you cannot see outside of you what you fail to see inside."
-Anthony de Mello- "The Power of Intention"

The deeper the self-realization of man, the more he influences the whole universe by his subtle spiritual vibrations, and the less he himself is affected by the phenomenal flux.
-Swami Sri Yukteswar tells Paramahansa Yogananda in "Autobiography of a Yogi."

Send out judgment and low energy, and that is what you'll attract back. Remember, when you judge another, you do not define them. You define yourself as someone who needs to judge. The same applies to judgments directed at you.
-Dr. Wayne Dyer- "The Power of Intention"

When you are inspired by a great purpose, everything will begin to work for you. Inspiration comes from moving back in spirit and connecting to the seven faces of intention. When you feel inspired, what appeared to be risky becomes a path you feel compelled to follow. The risks are gone because you're following your bliss, which is the truth within you. This is really love working in harmony with your intention.
-Dr. Wayne Dyer- "The Power of Intention"

Remind yourself that when you think about what you resent, you act upon what you think about, while simultaneously attracting more of it to you. Give your ego a reminder that you'll no longer opt to be offended or need to be right.
-Dr. Wayne Dyer- "The Power of Intention"

DEATH, DYING, & LIVING

Birth is the condition of having no past Death is the condition of having no future. Thus, the present moment, having no past or future, is simultaneously dead and alive. Birth & Death = the same timeless moment.
-Ken Wilber- "Spectrum of consciousness"

The rapture that is associated with being alive Is what it's all about.
-Joseph Campbell- "The Power of Myth"

Death, if we really face it, is about living. Living, if we really understand it, is about dying. This is the paradoxical koan the Tibetan Buddhist Lama tells us: From the moment we are born, we're moving towards our demise. Thus, life is considered precious for we never know when we'll lose it. Acknowledging death means celebrating life and vice versa.
-Andrew Blake-

People who would never think of suicide or ending their lives would think nothing of dribbling their lives away in useless minutes and hours every day.
-Thomas Carlyle-

Don't forget until it's too late that the business of life is not business but living.
-Forbes-

Life = indefinitely continued individuality.
-Franklin Merrel-Wolff- "Pathways Through To Space"

Life purpose is not something we discover, It's something we decide.
-Neale Donald Walsh- "Eye for the future" (1999 interview: Feb. issue)

I have heard it said that illness is an attempt to escape the truth. I suspect it is actually an attempt to embody the whole truth.
-Kat Duff- "Alchemy of Illness"

Pain is the sword that clears everything away.
-Kat Duff- "Alchemy of Illness"

Once in a while, pain gives way, like a trapdoor, into a hidden pool of grace. I lie perfectly still when it happens because I am afraid to believe it is true, and suspicious enough to think that a small tilt of my head or twist of my foot could dispel this miraculous state of grace. In that sudden stillness and unexpected calm, everything around me – the spider slipping into a crack in the wall, the twig scratching my window – seems to partake of an enduring perfection.
-Kat Duff- "Alchemy of Illness"

There is a curious paradox that surrounds pain: Nothing is more certain to those afflicted, while nothing is more open to question and doubt by others.
-Kat Duff- "Alchemy of Illness"

Illness is an opportunity for enlightenment. Illness is such a good means for eliminating toxins, the ingrained poisons

of our physical, mental, and emotional anguish.
-Kat Duff- "Alchemy of Illness"

Sick people often speak of having to drop the masks and roles they have assumed for the sake of others.
-Kat Duff- "Alchemy of Illness"

Illness is a process of transformation.
-Kat Duff- "Alchemy of Illness"

Decay is the beginning of all birth.
-Paracelsus-

We are all healed by our disease.
-Thomas Moore-

We are all free only when we no longer require health, however much we may prefer it.
-Arthur Frank- "At the Will of the Body"

It takes the ill person time to realize there is nothing and no one to bargain with.
-Arthur Frank- "At the Will of the Body"

Of course, the problem is not that I or any other ill person has "lost" control; the problem is that society's ideal of controlling the body is wrong in the first place. Control, or at least management, becomes a medical idea.
-Arthur Frank- "At the Will of the Body"

I have never heard an ill person praised for how well she or he expressed fear or grief, or was openly sad.
-Arthur Frank- "At the Will of the Body"

Medicine assumes that the person who has the disease is the only one who is ill. Illness is an experience shared by all who come into contact with the ill person.
-Arthur Frank- "At the Will of the Body"

In illness, there are no "negative emotions," only experiences that have to be lived through.
-Arthur Frank- "At the Will of the Body"

As little as we know of illness, we know even less of care.
-Arthur Frank- "At the Will of the Body"

The responsibility of the ill person is not to get well, but to express their illness well.
-Arthur Frank- "At the Will of the Body"

The art of medicine consists of amusing the patient while nature cures the disease.
-Voltaire-

Therefore, take a bold resolution and start to train seriously. As from today, you should dwell in singleness of thought; your eyes and ears should disengage from their object, regulate your diet, reduce your sleep; refrain from futile talk and jokes; stop thinking and worrying; cast away soft comfort and cease to discriminate between the

handsome and ugly so that you can become like the cicada feeding on dew to preserve its unsullied body and like the tortoise absorbing vitality from sunlight to enjoy a long life.
-Lu K'uan Yu- "Taoist Yoga"

Whenever one deems that one's life has been fulfilled, one can utilize death as a portal away from this existence.
-Deng Ming-Dao- "365 Tao"

The realized man is freed from the karma of past actions, save the karma that has already "sprouted," and is the causal power which maintains the continuance of the current gross body.
-Franklin Merrel-Wolff- "Pathways Through to Space"

Death will be known as a transition to a dimension that is increasingly familiar and non-threatening. Eventually, as the quantum energy patterns of our bodies begin to increase to ever higher levels, we will find ourselves in purely spiritual form.
-James Redfield- "The Celestine Vision"

An outside healer, however dramatic his methods, can really do no more than two very simple things: He can remove any obstacles to healing that are present and he can motivate the patient to get well.
-Andrew Weil- "The Natural Mind"

The Buddhist nirvana is a center of peace. Buddhism is a psychological religion. It starts with the psychological problem of suffering: All life is sorrowful; there is, however, an escape from sorrow; the escape is nirvana – which is a state of mind or consciousness, not a place somewhere, like Heaven. It is right here, in the midst of the turmoil of life. It is the state you find when you are no longer driven to live by compelling desires, fears, and social commitments. When you have found your center of freedom you can act by choice out of that. Voluntary action out of this center is the action of the Bodhisattvas – joyful participation in the sorrows of the world. You are not grabbed, because you have released yourself from the grabbers of fear, lust, and duties. These are the rulers of the world. There is an instructive Tibetan Buddhist painting in which the so-called "wheel of becoming" is represented. In monasteries, this painting would appear inside the cloister but on the outer wall. What is shown is the mind's image of the world when still caught in the grip of fear of the lord of death. Six realms are represented as spokes of the ever-revolving wheel: One is of animal life, another of the Gods in Heaven, another of human life, and a fourth of the souls being punished in hell. A fifth realm is of the belligerent demons, antigods or titans. And the sixth is of the hungry ghosts, the souls of those in whose love for others there was attachment, clinging, and expectation. The hungry ghosts have enormous ravenous bellies and pinpoint mouths. However, in the midst of these realms, there is a Buddha, signifying the possibility of release and illumination.

-Joseph Campbell- "The Power of Myth"

Robert Lowell wrote, "Sometimes I am weak enough to enter Heaven." When you are weak enough, you let go, and that is when you find the rose. That is when you know that it is not you living your life. It is the divine. It is not you who are doing anything. You do not exist in the way you think you do. You are a wave on the great ocean of energy and that ocean is carrying you at every moment. But you are also that ocean because being a wave, what else could you be but the sea? You are the rose you find, and that rose is blossoming in everything, always.
-Andrew Harvey- (on Rumi) "The Way of Passion"

There is perfection in everything. Need nothing, desire everything. Choose what shows up. Feel your feelings. Cry your cries. Laugh your laughs. Honor your truths. In a moment of great tragedy, the challenge is always to quiet the mind and move deep within the soul. You automatically do this when you have no control over it. Have you ever talked with a person who accidentally ran a car off a bridge? Or found himself facing a gun? Or nearly drowned? Often they will tell you that they were overcome by a curious calm, time slowed way down, and there was no fear at all.
-Neale Donald Walsh- "Conversations with God"

When the angel of death approaches, it is terrible. When he reaches you, it is bliss.
-Joseph Campbell- "The Power of Myth"

Plato said that a philosopher prepares for death by freeing the soul to contemplate eternal bliss.
-Thomas Moore- "Soul Mates"

Remember that you belong to no one and no one belongs to you. Reflect that someday you will suddenly leave everything in this world – so make the acquaintance of God now.
-Paramahansa Yogananda- "Autobiography of a Yogi"

We are also beginning to recognize that sickness is a relative term, as is normality. One may express the symptoms of a psychic sickness by being sane, normal, and well-adjusted to a sick society.
-Liz Green- "Saturn"

Under the impact of the unfamiliar and the altogether real danger of my physical annihilation, my body had to make use of its hidden resources, or die. The trick seemed to be in the truthful acceptance of the possibility that such resources exist and can be reached.
-Carlos Castenada- "The Second Ring of Power"

SUGGESTED LITERATURE:

- Superconsciousness: J. Donald Walters
- The Power of Imagination: The Neville Goddard Treasury (and other books by) Neville Goddard Author: Neville Goddard
- It Works: The Little Red Book: RHJ
- Acres of Diamonds: Russell H. Conwell
- As a Man Thinketh: James Allen
- See You At The Top: Zig Ziglar
- The Magic of Thinking Big: David J. Schwartz
- The Magic of Believing: Claude M. Bristol
- The Law of Success in Sixteen Lessons: Napoleon Hill
- How to Win Friends and Influence People: Dale Carnegie
- Map of Consciousness (and other books by): David R. Hawkins
- The Biology Of Belief: Unleashing The Power Of Consciousness, Matter & Miracles (and other books by): Bruce H. Lipton, Ph.D.
- Take Off Your Glasses and See: A Mind/Body Approach to Expanding Your Eyesight and Insight (and other books by): Jacob Liberman
- First Steps to Higher Yoga: Swami Vyas Dev Ji
- Beyond the Quantum: Michael Talbot
- Beyond Einstein: Dr. Michio Kaku & Jennifer Trainer
- Black Holes & Time Warps: Kip S. Thorne
- Quantum Healing: Deepak Chopra
- The Natural Mind: Andrew Weil
- The Marriage of the Sun and Moon: Andrew Weil
- Pathways Through to Space: Franklin Merrel-Wolff
- The Power of Myth: Joseph Campbell
- A Brief History of Time: Stephen W. Hawking
- Through Time Into Healing: Brian L. Weiss

- The Alchemy of Illness: Kat Duff
- Zen Word, Zen Calligraphy: Eido Tai Shimano & Kogetsu Tani
- Tao Te Ching: Lao Tsu (Jane English version)
- The Bubishi: Patrick McCarthy
- Classical Man: Richard Kim
- The Tao of Jeet Kune Do: Bruce Lee
- The Tao of Health, Sex & Longevity: Daniel Reid
- Healing Love Through the Tao: Mantak & Maneewan Chia (Two books; one for men, one for women: read both)
- The Celestine Prophecy: James Redfield
- Spectrum of Consciousness: Ken Wilber
- Autohypnosis: Ronald Shone
- Shamanism: Archaic Techniques of Ecstasy: Mircea Eliade
- The Way of the Shaman: Michael Harner
- Medicine Woman book series
- (and other books by): Lynn Andrews
- Kryon; the End Times & Don't Think Like a Human: Kryon
- The Doctrine of Vibration: Mark S. G. Dyczkowski
- The Mozart Effect: Don Campbell
- The Tao of Physics: Fritjof Capra
- The Tao of Music and Sound Psychology: John M. Ortiz
- Conversations with God: Neale Donald Walsh
- Decoding the Secret Language of Your Body: Martin Rush
- Care of the Soul: Thomas Moore
- Subtle Energy: William Collinge
- The Tao of Sexology: Dr. Stephen Chang
- The Great Tao: Dr. Stephen Chang

- Chronicles of the Tao: Deng Ming-Dao
- The Art of the Bedchamber: Douglas Wile
- Taoist Health Exercise Book: Da Liu
- The Tao of Health & Longevity: Da Liu
- How to Think Like Leonardo Da Vinci: Michael Gelb
- Mutant Message Down Under: Marlo Morgan
- Autobiography of a Yogi: Paramahansa Yogananda
- Radha; Diary of a Woman's Search: Swami Sivananda Radha
- Mantras; Words of Power: Swami Sivananda Radha
- Asana, Pranayama, Mudra and Bandha (and other books by) Saraswati Satyananda Swami
- The Writings of Francis Scovel Shinn: Francis Scovel Shinn
- Rich Dad, Poor Dad: Robert Kiyosaki
- Indigo Children: Lee Carol & Jan Tober
- The Essential Rumi: Coleman Barks
- Gandhi:The Story of my experiments with Truth: an autobiography
- The Bhagavad Gita: Swami Sivananda version
- The Classical Illustrated Book of Yoga: Swami Sivananda

SUGGESTED AUTHORS:

- J. Krishnamurti Coomaraswami
- Andrew Weil
- Stephen Chang
- Franklin Merrel-Wolff
- Marlo Morgan
- Michael Talbot
- Paulo Coelho
- Den Ming-Dao
- Thomas Moore
- Joseph Campbell
- Robert Kiyosaki
- Daniel Reid
- Kip S. Thorne
- Mantak Chia
- Mircea Eliade
- Rumi
- Noam Chomsky
- William Blake
- Michael Tierra
- Basho
- Robert svoboda
- Abhinavagupta
- David Frawley
- Maya Tiwari
- Richard Kim
- Brian Weiss
- Jung Chang
- Fritjof Capra
- Swami Sivananda
- Paramahansa Yogananda
- Richard Bach
- Neale Donald Walsh
- Francis Scovel Shinn
- Carolyn Myss
- Dr. Wayne Dyer
- Swami Vishnu Devananda
- Swami Vivekananda
- Swami Sivananda Radha

www.ingramcontent.com/pod-product-compliance
Lightning Source LLC
Chambersburg PA
CBHW051957290426
44110CB00015B/2286